Next Generation
ENERGY

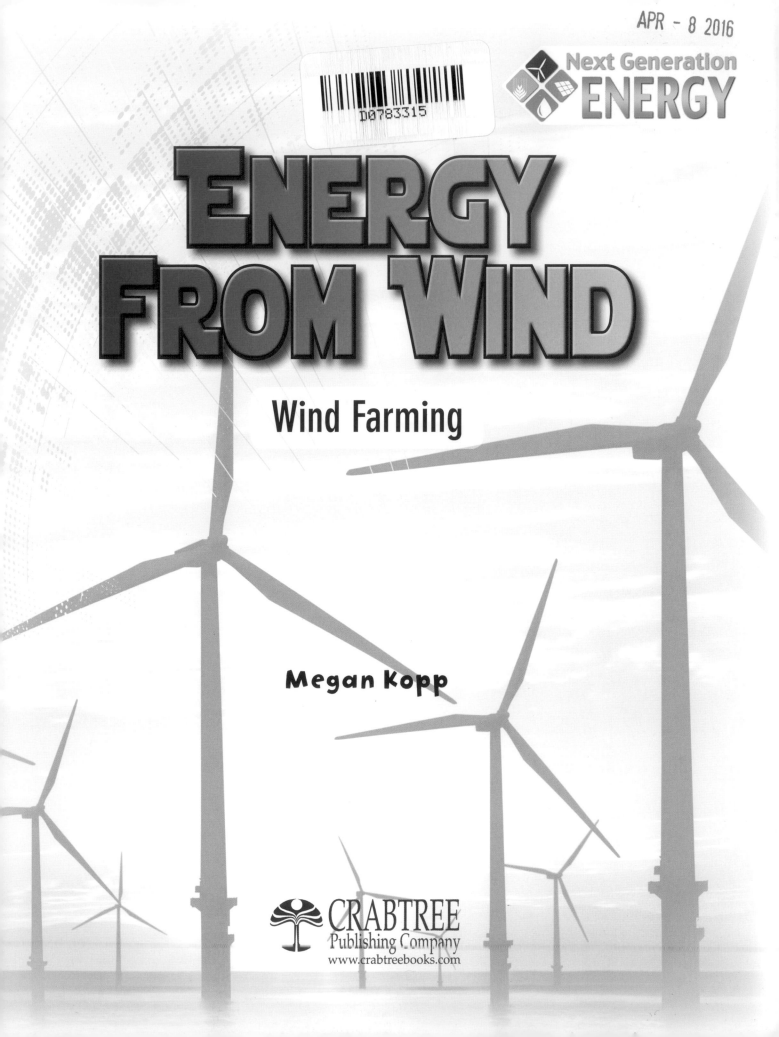

ENERGY FROM WIND

Wind Farming

Megan Kopp

CRABTREE
Publishing Company
www.crabtreebooks.com

Crabtree Publishing Company

www.crabtreebooks.com

Author: Megan Kopp

Editors: Sarah Eason, Jen Sanderson, and Shirley Duke

Proofreader: Katie Dicker and Wendy Scavuzzo

Editorial director: Kathy Middleton

Design: Paul Myerscough and Geoff Ward

Cover design: Paul Myerscough

Photo research: Sarah Eason and Jen Sanderson

Prepress technician: Margaret Amy Salter

Print coordinator: Margaret Amy Salter

Consultant: Richard Spilsbury, degree in Zoology, 30 years as an author and editor of educational science books

Written and produced for Crabtree Publishing by Calcium Creative

Photo Credits:

t=Top, bl=Bottom Left, br=Bottom Right

Dreamstime: Toa555: p. 11; Shutterstock: Africa924: p. 18; American Spirit: pp. 8–9; 20–21; Anton Foltin: p. 16; Artjazz: pp. 7, 26–27; Asier Romero: p. 28; Atomazul: p. 4; Bildagentur Zoonar GmbH: pp. 24–25; Chungking: pp. 16–17; David Lee p. 20; Elena Elisseeva: p. 6; EpicStockMedia: p. 22; Everett Historical: p. 8; Fedor Selivanov: pp. 3, 9; Felix Lipov: p. 26; Gallinago Media: p. 25; Goodluz: p. 12; Gualtiero Boffi: pp. 3, 18–19; HildaWeges Photography: pp. 28–29; Iakov Filimonov: pp. 24, 27; Igor K+isselev: p. 13; KKimages: pp. 10–11; Lester Balajadia: pp. 6–7; Maridav p. 21; Matyas Rehak: p. 17; Paul Prescott: pp. 22–23, 30–31; Ssuaphotos: p. 1; T Photography: p. 10; T.W. van Urk: p. 23; Tony Moran: pp. 14–15; Tory Kallman: p. 15; V. Schlichting: p. 14; Vibe Images pp. 4–5; Wikimedia Commons: Erik (HASH) Hersman: p. 19; Z22: pp. 12–13, 32.

Cover: Shutterstock: Ssuaphotos.

Library and Archives Canada Cataloguing in Publication

Kopp, Megan, author
    Energy from wind : wind farming / Megan Kopp.

(Next generation energy)
Includes index.
Issued in print and electronic formats.
ISBN 978-0-7787-1983-0 (bound).--
ISBN 978-0-7787-2006-5 (paperback).--
ISBN 978-1-4271-1641-3 (pdf).--
ISBN 978-1-4271-1633-8 (html)

    1. Wind power--Juvenile literature. 2. Wind power plants--Juvenile literature. 3. Renewable energy sources--Juvenile literature. 4. Clean energy--Juvenile literature. I. Title.

TJ820.K67 2015   j333.9'2   C2015-903222-9
                               C2015-903223-7

Library of Congress Cataloging-in-Publication Data

Kopp, Megan, author.
  Energy from wind : wind farming / Megan Kopp.
    pages cm. -- (Next generation energy)
  Includes index.
  ISBN 978-0-7787-1983-0 (reinforced library binding : alk. paper) --
ISBN 978-0-7787-2006-5 (pbk. : alk. paper) --
ISBN 978-1-4271-1641-3 (electronic pdf) --
ISBN 978-1-4271-1633-8 (electronic html)
1. Wind power--Juvenile literature. 2. Power resources--Juvenile literature. 3. Clean energy industries--Juvenile literature. 4. Wind power plants--Juvenile literature. I. Title.

TJ820.K67 2016
333.9'2--dc23
                   2015020963

Crabtree Publishing Company

www.crabtreebooks.com   1-800-387-7650

                Printed in Canada/082015/BF20150630

Published in Canada
Crabtree Publishing
616 Welland Ave.
St. Catharines, Ontario
L2M 5V6

Published in the United States
Crabtree Publishing
PMB 59051
350 Fifth Avenue, 59th Floor
New York, New York 10118

Published in the United Kingdom
Crabtree Publishing
Maritime House
Basin Road North, Hove
BN41 1WR

Published in Australia
Crabtree Publishing
3 Charles Street
Coburg North
VIC, 3058

Contents

What Is Energy?

We use energy for everything we do—from getting up in the morning to taking the bus to school to using our computers and smartphones in the evening. Understanding energy we use improves the chances that we will not waste this valuable resource.

Energy is the ability to do work. We use energy to move from place to place. We use energy to heat and light our homes. Energy comes in many different forms. **Mechanical energy** allows us to move things with simple machines such as wheels, gears, levers, and pulleys. **Chemical energy** is released when different substances react to each other. **Nuclear energy** is created when **atoms** are split apart in large reactors.

Change Is in the Wind

Like a superhero, energy can **transform**, or change, from one type to another but it cannot be created or destroyed. **Potential** energy is stored energy. When it is moving to do work, it is **kinetic** energy. Energy can come from nonrenewable and renewable resources.

Chicago, Illinois, is lit up at night. People in almost 50 buildings in the city have joined a program to reduce their energy use by 20 percent over the next five years.

Wind Power from Each Continent

- Asia 118,847 MW
- Africa 1,629 MW
- North America 71,411 MW
- South America 4,093 MW
- Europe 118,949 MW
- Australia 3,806 MW
- Antarctica 1 MW

This map shows wind energy usage around the world. Which continents have little or no wind power? Why might this be so in those countries?

Renewable resources include solar energy from the Sun, wind energy, geothermal energy from heat inside Earth, biomass power from plants, and hydroelectricity from flowing water. Renewable and nonrenewable resources can be used to produce electricity.

Energy Use and Pollution

Nonrenewable resources come from **fossil fuels** such as oil, natural gas, and coal, as well as uranium, which is used in nuclear power. Burning fossil fuels to create electricity has the downside of polluting the environment with **carbon dioxide** and other **greenhouse gases**. These gases are directly related to climate change. As a result, there is a lot of interest in renewable resources.

REWIND

Hundreds of years ago, our ancestors used fire to provide heat and to cook their food. When the Sun went down, they built up the fire or went to sleep. As populations continued to grow, firewood became scarce and people had to go farther to gather the resource. What would your neighborhood look like if everyone still used wood fires today?

5

All About Wind

The Sun is the biggest source of energy on Earth. Energy from the Sun can be collected directly using solar panels to produce electricity, but it can also be used indirectly when it changes into wind. In theory, all of the wind energy available around the world could provide 13 times more electricity than is currently generated, or produced.

When the Sun comes up, the air over the land heats up faster than air over oceans and other large bodies of water. The heated air is lighter and so it rises. The cooler air is **denser**, and it falls and replaces the air over the land. At night, the reverse happens. Air over the water is warmer and rises, where it is replaced by cooler air from land. As air falls and rises, a difference in **pressure** is created. Pressure is the force produced when something presses or pushes against something else. Air moves from areas of high pressure to areas of low pressure. This creates wind.

Lake Superior is the largest of the Great Lakes. It absorbs huge amounts of heat in the summer and slowly releases it in the winter. This creates a **microclimate** involving wind and moisture.

Blow Me Away

Patterns of wind flow are affected by the **terrain**, or type of land, bodies of water, and **vegetation**. Wind energy is also affected by other factors. Air currents move faster and more consistently at higher **altitudes**. The jet stream is a current of fast-moving air found in the upper levels of the atmosphere. Wind also gathers energy when it moves over long distances without any obstacles in the way. This is why flat regions, such as the prairies, can have extremely high winds.

Only some regions are so gusty they generate enough wind energy to power **turbines** and produce enough electricity to make a **profit**, or make money. In the United States, the plains region, which runs north to south between the Rockies and the Appalachians, produces the most wind energy. In Canada, great wind generation areas include southern Alberta, the coasts of the Great Lakes, and the Gaspe Peninsula.

Earth's surface can slow down wind. Open water allows winds to blow stronger and more consistently.

The Energy Future: You Choose

In 2001, the first **offshore** wind farm in the United States was planned. With 130 turbines just 5 miles (8 km) off the Massachusetts coast, the farm would supply 75 percent of electricity demand for Cape Cod, Martha's Vineyard, and Nantucket. Opponents said it would negatively impact the **ecosystem**, local fisheries, tourism, property values, and more. Many environmental impact studies, nine years, and more than $30 million later, the Cape Wind project was approved. Yet, in 2015, the project was still stuck in legal battles. Do you think Cape Wind should keep pushing for development?

Time for Wind Power

Sailboats have been using wind power for thousands of years and the first-known windmill dates back to 700 CE in Persia. Windmills were being used in China by 1200. Around 200 years later, Holland became a world design trendsetter. The Dutch used windmills to help pump water out of low-lying, marshy areas to allow for farming.

Early windmills had four blades and a **weather vane**, or tail, to turn the device into the wind. These windmills were used to grind wheat, corn, and other grains, as well as for pumping water and cutting wood in sawmills. The first windmill in the United States was designed by Daniel Halladay in 1854. Windmills became a popular way to pump water on the western frontier. Between 1850 and 1970, more than 6 million mechanical windmills were working across the United States.

From Mill to Turbine

Windmills are the grandparents of today's modern wind turbines. When electrical devices were invented, people started using wind to generate electricity. In 1887, Charles F. Brush put up the first wind-powered electric **generator** in Cleveland, Ohio. It powered his home for many years.

Before the **Industrial Revolution**, wool was spun by hand. Power provided by water mills allowed textile factories, such as American Woolen Company, to expand.

As power lines began stringing out across the countryside, the demand for a local power source dipped. It was not until the oil crisis in the early 1970s that wind energy was again considered. California led the way. From 1981 to 1986, 15,000 turbines dotted the landscape. During the 1990s, California produced half of the world's wind power. This amount was only 2,200 **megawatts** (MW). A megawatt is a unit for measuring power that is equal to 1 million **watts**. An average light bulb uses 60 watts.

Now Europe Leads the Way

In 1982, a European **delegation** toured California to look at the wind energy market. A small number of turbines were exported and the European Wind Energy Association was formed. The following year, 10 times as many turbines were shipped to Europe and installed. By 2000, Europe had become the world leader in wind power.

Historic Dutch windmills provided a home for the windsmith with separate floors for grinding and storing grain produced.

REWIND

During the Industrial Revolution in the 1700s and 1800s, the demand for energy to support new factories grew. Nonrenewable resources such as fossil fuels provided reliable energy, but at a cost. Burning fossil fuels release harmful greenhouse gases such as carbon dioxide. Carbon dioxide levels in the atmosphere have increased from 280 parts per million (ppm) to 385 ppm in the last 150 years. **Clean energy** sources are urgently needed. Discuss early windmills and what their uses were at that time in relation to today's energy needs.

Talking About Turbines

Wind turbines are tall, tube-shaped towers with rotating blades at the top. When the blades move, they turn a generator and create electricity. The turbine converts kinetic energy of the wind into mechanical energy, which the generators transform into electricity.

It takes an average wind speed of 14 miles per hour (23 kph) to convert wind energy to electricity. The problem is that wind is seldom constant. If the wind blows too hard, the turbine risks being damaged. If it blows too lightly, the blades will not turn.

Straight Up Facts

Most wind turbines are horizontal axis, such as farm windmills used for pumping water. With horizontal-axis turbines, three large blades spin parallel to the tower. Less common vertical-axis turbines spin like an eggbeater. In vertical-axis machines, the main **rotor** and generator are near the ground. This makes maintenance easier and cheaper.

These windmills on display at the American Wind Power Center museum in Lubbock, Texas, were designed to pump water.

Wind turbines come in many sizes and power ratings. Small, home-sized turbines are less than 50 **kilowatts** (kW) in size. Utility-scale, horizontal-axis turbines range from 50 to 750 kW. They stand about 200 to 300 feet (61 to 91 m) high. The largest machines have blades that are longer than the length of a football field. The blades make 10 to 20 rotations a minute, and can produce enough electricity to power hundreds of homes. The towers and blades are painted white to make them visible to low-flying aircraft. A large grouping of turbines on a wind farm is often called an **array**.

Engineers have tried to make these vertical-axis helix wind turbines more attractive by making them look like flowers.

FAST FORWARD

What flutters like leaves on a tree, looks like modern art, and generates electricity? It is a new vertical wind turbine that is about to be "planted" on the streets of Paris, France. These unique tree turbines put out 3.1 kW of power. The turbines spin silently and can move with winds as low as 4.4 mph (7 kph). This is twice as sensitive as a conventional turbine. Each wind tree produces enough power to light up 15 streetlights. Why do you think people might prefer tree turbines to traditional wind turbines? Give reasons for your answer.

Farming the Wind

Wind farms are simply a group of wind turbines put together to make a single wind power plant. Most of the world's wind energy comes from wind farms. They can range in size from a handful to hundreds of turbines. Building wind farms requires careful planning. Studies must be made as to how often the wind blows at the site.

Wind turbines have to be positioned correctly to take advantage of wind speed and direction. They must also be located at the right **elevation**, or height, to catch the most wind. Large-scale wind farms are often seen on high, exposed plateaus, ridges, islands, and flat agricultural lands.

Engineers are constantly working to improve the performance of wind turbines and the generators that change wind energy into electricity.

First and Foremost

The world's first wind farm was built in 1980 on the shoulder of Crotched Mountain in southern New Hampshire. It included 20 wind turbines, each capable of producing 30 kW of power. The Cowley Ridge wind plant, built in southern Alberta in 1993, was Canada's first **commercial**, or money-making, wind farm. It had 52 wind turbines along the 1.6-mile (2.5 km) ridge in one of the country's windiest spots.

Many of the largest **onshore** wind farms can be found in the United States. In 2013, more than 30 states had large-scale wind power projects. The Alta Wind Energy Center in California was the largest wind farm in the United States in 2014. The farm generated more than enough electricity to power 450,000 homes.

Protestors sometimes march against industrial wind turbine farms being developed too close to their homes.

The Energy Future: You Choose

Wind farms span hundreds, and even thousands, of acres (hectares). They are often located in agricultural areas. The land between the turbines can still be used for farming. Cattle and other grazing livestock seem to be unaffected by turbines. However, wind farms are often on ridge tops or across wide open flatlands, so they can be a visual concern—especially as the number of wind farms continues to grow. Should there be a limit on the number and size of wind farms? Discuss your answer.

Offshore Breezes

Wind farms can also be found off the coastlines of many countries. Called offshore wind farms, these turbines take advantage of the stronger and more frequent offshore winds. When air flows over open water, it tends to move more quickly because there are no hills or trees to block the flow, and it blows more steadily. Another advantage to building offshore is that the project does not take up valuable land space.

Offshore wind farms are located at least 1 mile (1.6 km) or more away from the coast, in water that is up to 98 feet (30 m) deep. Offshore turbines tend to be larger, with higher towers and longer blades than those found on land. In the same way that oil and gas drilling platforms are built, steel poles are driven deep into the seabed. The turbines are specially manufactured to withstand high wind, strong tides, and potential **ice jams**. Ice jams occur when water builds up behind an ice blockage. The turbines are linked by underwater power lines to the coast.

The average expected cost of a new offshore wind farm is more than $2 million per MW.

Setting the Mark

The first-ever commercial offshore wind farm was built in Denmark in 1991. Sitting 1.2 miles (1.9 km) off the coastline, it has 11 450-kW wind turbines. Today, most operational wind farms can be found in the North Sea. Strong, consistent winds are a key factor for the sites' success. One of the world's largest offshore wind farms is the London Array, 12 miles (19 km) off England's coast. It has 175 turbines and can generate enough power for 500,000 homes. The European Union, as a whole, has just over 8 **gigawatts** (GW) of offshore wind energy capacity.

Offshore wind farms are costly to develop and it can be risky putting up turbines in open water. Another downside of offshore wind farms is that developers need to drill into the seafloor to anchor the turbines. This has an impact on the **marine**, or ocean, wildlife. Although planners work to avoid shipping routes and harbors, large offshore wind farms still pose a potential risk for marine navigation.

Offshore site planners must consider the effects turbines might have on marine life such as Atlantic bottlenose dolphins.

The Energy Future: You Choose

Offshore wind farms do not take up valuable space on land. They can be larger and therefore provide more power. They are costly to build and can have an impact on the marine environment while they are being built. Overall, do you think offshore wind farms are effective, efficient, and an environmentally friendly method of generating electricity? Explain your reasoning. What part does technology play in establishing wind farms, and how has it helped or harmed the environment? Consider the objections that people might have to these offshore wind farms, too.

Where in the World?

The number of global wind energy projects has grown dramatically since the 1980s. Back then, California had 90 percent of the world's installed wind energy capacity. Today, China leads the world when it comes to wind energy capacity. At the end of 1997, the country had just 146 MW of wind power capacity. By the end of 2014, that number jumped to 114,763 MW. No other country comes close.

The United States is the second-highest wind-energy producer in the world, with 65,879 MW by the end of 2014. In Europe, Germany tops the list with close to 40,000 MW for 2014. Overall, there has been dramatic growth in wind power capacity over past 20 years, with no signs of slowing down. From Albania to Vietnam, wind power can now be found in more than 100 different countries.

Record Breaker

In 2014, Denmark set a new world record for wind-energy production. Just over 39 percent of its overall electricity came from wind power. In the United Kingdom, enough wind energy is generated to supply more than 6.7 million homes. Scotland's wind turbines provide almost all the electricity needed for its population. By 2030, the country's **power grid** could be fueled only by renewable resources.

The San Gorgonio Pass near Palm Springs is one of the windiest places in southern California.

Some Do, Some Don't

Wind power is used wherever there is enough strong, steady wind and enough money to pay for the projects. Developing a wind power industry is expensive and some countries cannot afford the technology. Lack of development can also come from a seemingly endless supply of nonrenewable resources, which are cheaper to use. A lack of political support to drive the development of renewable resources can also limit wind power.

China is surging forward because their normal energy sources will not be enough to meet their future needs. Germany, like many European countries, has strong public and political support for renewable energy. On the other hand, the United Arab Emirates had 1 MW of wind power capacity at the end of 2004. Eight years later, that number had not changed. With a surplus of wealth in nonrenewable resources, the drive to switch to the more expensive wind power is not as pressing.

Camels, used for hundreds of years for transportation, can be found in the Thar Desert in Rajasthan, India, alongside modern wind-energy technology.

The Energy Future: You Choose

Wind power and its related technology is expensive, but the fact that it is a free and renewable resource is driving change. Based on the information provided, do you think every country in the world should be actively pursuing wind farms, both on land and offshore? Give reasons for your answer. Support your answer with ideas from the book.

Powerful Tales

In 2002, William Kamkwamba was a 14-year-old school student in Malawi, Africa. His parents were farmers living in a small, rural village. When a severe drought hit their country, they could not afford food to eat, let alone find money for William to go to school.

The young teen was worried about falling behind and not being able to catch up when he returned to school. He started visiting a local library and homeschooling himself. It was at the library that he discovered an American fifth-grade textbook called *Using Energy*. The book showed a wind turbine on its cover and it caught his eye. Learning to read English, William read the book from cover to cover. It fed his curiosity for mechanical and electrical devices, and led to a life-changing project.

In poorer regions of Africa, some children cannot afford to go to school and must work to help support their families.

William the Windsmith

William decided he was going to build a windmill to bring power to his home because his village did not have this luxury. He wanted to be able to stay up and read after the Sun went down. He also thought he could use the windmill to bring up water from a well so that his father could water the crops. This would mean that they would have food all year round.

William started collecting scraps of metal, including an old bicycle frame, and began crafting a working windmill. The villagers thought he was crazy. There was no word in his language for windmill.

Overnight Hero

When William climbed the tower to set the windmill in motion and the energy made a light bulb shine, he became an instant hero. His work gained international attention and William was able to continue his education and expand the project to help his village.

William Kamkwamba refined the design of his first windmill moving from three blades to four to increase the power created.

FAST FORWARD

Creative minds such as William Kamkwamba's are changing the future. Others are also leading the way. Aerial wind turbines that float in the air like a tethered balloon are being studied. They are portable, can be controlled by computers, and do not require a great expense to be up and running. In faraway areas, imported fossil fuels for generators could be replaced with this cheaper energy source. Brainstorm a list of pros and cons for aerial wind farms. How does technology improve the lives of people in developing countries, and what are its limitations?

Spotlight on North America

The United States has enough untapped wind energy to produce 10 times the amount of electricity needed to supply the entire country. Although this resource varies from region to region, the overall source is there. At the start of 2014, the country had more than 48,000 operating wind turbines in 39 states. Currently, only 4.1 percent of the United States' overall electrical consumption is powered by wind.

Texas has the highest installed wind power capacity. In 2013, this was 14,098 MW, which is the same as powering 3,315,000 homes by wind. California comes in second, even though it has more individual wind turbines. The greenhouse-gas-saving benefit of this clean energy is equivalent to taking 1.3 million cars off the road. Iowa comes in third for installed wind power capacity and number of wind turbines. In 2013, wind energy was 27 percent of Iowa's electricity production.

In the late 1800s, small trestle towers topped with steel paddle-type blades were common windmills in the United States.

Canada and Mexico

In 2014, the province of Ontario was Canada's leader in wind energy with 1,852 wind turbines and an installed wind power capacity of 3,490 MW. That same year, Ontario became the first region in North America to cut coal as an electricity-generating resource. Quebec comes in second for Canadian wind power generation. The province produces enough electricity for more than 600,000 homes. Alberta ranks third for wind power.

Mexico is also showing growth in the wind power market. In 2014, the country had 1,370 MW of installed wind power capacity. It also has over 12,000 MW of potential capacity in new wind farms. Most of Mexico's wind energy production is found in the state of Oaxaca.

Montreal, Quebec, is home to many wind energy service providers, parts manufacturers, and project developers.

The Energy Future: You Choose

A recent project for two offshore wind turbines located 26 miles (42 km) off the coast of Virginia Beach, Virginia, has been derailed as a result of costs. The company estimated that the project would cost around $230 million to complete. The only construction bid the company received came in at almost double that amount. North Americans still rely on fossil fuels, but global **climate change** is pushing for the switch to renewable resources such as wind energy. Is there a limit to how much North America should spend on alternate energy sources? What is the consequence of failing to make the change? What do you think could be done to help reduce project costs?

Clean Power Positives

Wind energy and solar power are clean energy. These renewable resources are the fastest-growing energy sources worldwide. Wind power is the perfect green resource. It does not create any greenhouse gas emissions or radioactive waste. It uses almost no water. Clean energy sources reduce the need to use nonrenewable resources such as fossil fuels and nuclear energy.

Wind energy is free. The cost comes from harnessing the wind, but this cost is recovered over time, then the resource is truly free. Wind is available around the world and constantly being renewed. A unique feature of wind turbines is that they are available in a variety of sizes. This means that individuals as well as businesses have the opportunity to produce their own power. New technology is reducing the cost of wind power turbines while still increasing efficiency.

Wind powers our sails—and our homes—in an environmentally friendly fashion.

Blowing in the Wind

Wind energy does not need to be pulled out of the earth. Electricity is generated onsite and added into the electrical grid by way of power lines. No motorized vehicles are needed to haul the resource to another location for use.

Another benefit of wind energy is that the land where wind farms are established can be used for many purposes. The wind turbines are placed on high towers, so the land below can be used for growing crops. Livestock can graze on wind farms. Roadways and pipelines can be built through wind farms, which helps keep them contained and reduces habitat **fragmentation**.

Efficient land use can be seen where sheep graze below wind turbines on a dike in Netherlands.

REWIND

In the early 1940s, the first large-scale wind turbine, named Smith-Putnam, was built on a ridgetop called Grandpa's Knob in Vermont. The blades stretched 175 feet (53 m) across. It supplied power to a local town for 18 months, until one of the blades broke off. The project was canceled because the manufacturer did not think that wind turbines could supply enough energy to make money. What would the future of wind power look like today if that same thought still existed?

Wind Power Issues

While the pros far outweigh the cons, wind energy is not perfect. Electricity production from wind energy is expensive and is not reliable. Not everyone appreciates the look of a wind turbine in their backyard, and turbines are not silent. Wind farms can have an impact on the natural environment.

One of the biggest disadvantages of wind energy is that it is unpredictable. Wind does not blow on a regular schedule at set rates. Turbines can produce electricity only when the wind blows at the right speed. If the wind is too strong or too soft, the blades will not turn. Most turbines usually operate at a fraction of their actual capacity. For example, a 6 MW wind turbine typically produces only around 2 MW.

Some people object to the look of wind farms. They say that the industrial appearance of the steel towers spoils the landscape for people who live nearby, or those who are visiting the area to enjoy its beauty.

Wind turbines can dominate the landscape and forever change the view.

Wind turbines are not silent. Although modern technology has reduced sound levels, a working turbine still creates a certain amount of noise. Another minor negative is the possibility for **shadow flicker**. The blades of the rotor can cause shadows depending on the angle of the Sun. It can be bothersome but produces no harmful health effects. As with noise levels, the impact of shadow flicker can be reduced with proper location planning.

What About the Wildlife?

One of the biggest concerns about wind energy is the effect it has on wildlife and the environment. Any construction project or permanent human-made structure has an impact on local plants and animals. Depending on the area, this impact can be large or small. Planners of any wind farms must think carefully about the environment, and ongoing studies are looking at the impact wind turbines have on birds and bats. New blades spin only once every 15 minutes, so collisions are reduced.

Migrating birds such as geese can come into conflict with turbines when their migration paths take them through wind farms.

The Energy Future: You Choose

There are definite pluses to developing wind energy. There are also downsides to this renewable resource. People have strong opinions on both sides of the debate. There are people for and against expanding this alternative energy source. Do you think wind energy is good or bad for the environment and the life nearby? Support your answers with evidence from the book and explain your thinking.

Taking the Future by Storm

Wind energy is one of the largest, fastest, and cheapest ways to cut greenhouse gases and help reduce climate change. The 2014 Global Wind Energy Outlook shows that wind power could reach 2,000 GW by 2030, supplying about 17 to 19 percent of global electricity. This would create more than a million new jobs. By 2050, wind power could provide 25 to 30 percent of global electricity supply.

This power plant in the state of New York uses natural gas, fuel oil, and kerosene to generate electricity.

Energy companies are responsible for almost half of all carbon dioxide emissions and about one quarter of other greenhouse gas emissions. Clean energy such as wind and solar power will reduce 3.8 billion tons (3.5 billion metric tons) of carbon dioxide emissions each year by 2030. Wind energy also reduces sulfur dioxide emissions by 347 million pounds (157 million kg) per year and nitrous oxide emissions by 214 million pounds (97 million kg) per year. These **pollutants** contribute to **acid rain** and smog.

Winding Up

The United States is gearing up to make wind power 20 percent of its electrical generation by 2030. Canada's national wind power vision is to supply 20 percent of its electricity needs by 2025. The Danish government aims to get half of its electricity from wind power by 2020, and all of it from renewable energy by 2050. Over 500,000 Europeans will be employed by wind power companies by 2020. By 2030, this number will jump by more than 250,000 and more than half of these jobs will be in offshore wind energy production.

Offshore is the future of wind power. While projects such as Cape Wind are still on hold in the United States, other major projects are taking flight. Deepwater Wind has the funding to build a small, five-turbine wind farm off the coast of Block Island in Rhode Island. It will provide power for 17,000 homes. The company expects it to be operational by the end of 2016.

Northern wildlife species, like this polar bear, really are on thin ice when it comes to global climate change.

FAST FORWARD

Changes in how the world generates electricity are needed if we are to have a chance of keeping the global temperature rise to 36°F (2°C) or less. Reducing greenhouse gas emissions seems to be the key, but we need to act now. If we do not, climate change will cause the loss of glacial ice, rising sea levels, and drastic changes to our weather patterns. Are we doing enough with clean energy, such as wind power, to make a difference? Discuss your answers. Why do you think people are reluctant to use renewable resources? Explain your thinking.

Power Up!

People have been harnessing wind power for thousands of years. From sailing ships to windmills, wind energy has been a driving force. Today, huge wind turbines capture the wind in green farms that provide electricity to power many homes and businesses. Engineers work hard to find the proper location for the right size and shape of wind turbine.

What Can You Do?

Designing wind turbines involves many factors. Energy production can vary depending on the location, height of the tower, shape of the blades, length of the blades, and the number of blades. Although they are more complicated than windmills, all wind turbines have a tower, blades, and axle. You can learn about how they work together by building your own model windmill. You can also test location distances from the wind source and use different blade sizes to see which one works best.

Using the information in this book, what factors would you consider if you were planning a wind farm?

Activity

Build your own model wind turbine and test it to see how it captures the wind.

You Will Need:

- empty, clean, cardboard milk carton
- 1 cup sand
- Tape
- A pen
- A ruler
- A drinking straw
- A paper clip
- Scissors
- A coin
- Two brass fasteners
- String
- Three circles of cardstock cut 4, 6, and 8 inches (10, 15, and 20 cm) in diameter
- An electric fan

1. Pour the sand into the milk carton. Tape the spout closed.
2. On the center of one side of the milk carton, poke a hole 1.2 inches (3 cm) down from the top edge. Do the same on the opposite side of the carton.
3. Insert a straw through the holes with equal lengths sticking out on either side.
4. Tie one end of the string to a paperclip and tape the other end to one end of the straw. The string should hang to the side of the straw, not over the end.
5. Choose one of the cardstock circles and trace the coin at the center.
6. Divide each circle into quarters. Cut along the four lines. Do not cut into the inner circle.
7. Fold each section of the circle in half so that half of each section stands up.
8. Push a brass fastener though the center of each of the inner circles.
9. Tape the fastener from the end of one of the turbine blade circles onto the empty end of the straw.
10. Place the turbine with the string and paperclip hanging over the edge of a table. Turn on the fan and record how fast the string winds up the paperclip.

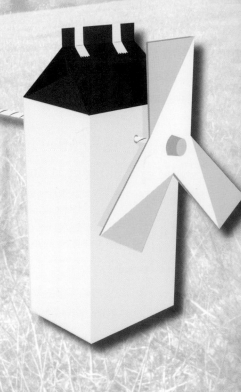

What Do You Think?

Try your windmill with all three blades. Does the size of the blade make a difference to the speed at which the string winds up? How important do you think it is for wind turbine engineers to find the right blade size? Explain your thoughts.

Glossary

Please note: Some bold-faced words are defined where they appear in the text

acid rain Rainfall made sufficiently acidic from polluting emissions and gases that it causes environmental harm

altitudes Heights

array An ordered arrangement

atoms The smallest possible parts of an element

carbon dioxide A gas molecule made up of a carbon atom joined with two oxygen atoms

climate change The increase in the temperature of the atmosphere near Earth's surface that can contribute to changes in global climate patterns

clean energy Energy that emits fewer or no greenhouse gases

delegation A group of people chosen to act on someone else's behalf

denser More crowded or massed together for each unit of space

ecosystem The plants, animals, and other organisms that live together in a specific environment

fossil fuels Energy sources made from the remains of plants and animals that died millions of years ago and were buried

fragmentation Patches of habitat resulting from cutting down forest and clearing land

generator A machine that changes motion into electrical energy

gigawatts (GW) Units of measure for energy; There are 1 billion watts in a gigawatt.

greenhouse gases Gases in the atmosphere that contribute to the greenhouse effect

Industrial Revolution A rapid change in which countries become more focused on using machines to make goods

kilowatts Units of measure for energy; There are 1,000 watts in a kilowatt.

kinetic Relating to or resulting from motion or movement

microclimate A small zone where the climate differs from the surrounding area

migrating When animals and birds move from one location to another in search of food, water, and breeding opportunities

offshore In the ocean, some distance from the land

onshore On land

pollutants Materials that are released into the environment and are harmful or poisonous to plants, animals, or people

potential Having the capacity to develop into something in the future

power grid A network of transmission lines that takes electricity from power plants to consumers

radioactive waste The leftover materials from nuclear power that continue to emit radiation, which is highly dangerous

rotor The rotating assembly in a wind turbine

shadow flicker The flickering effect caused when moving wind turbine blades cast alternating shadows

turbines Machines with rotating blades

watts Unit of measure for energy

vegetation Types of plants and trees

Learning More

Find out more about energy and wind power.

Books

Bailey, Diane. *Harnessing Energy: Wind Power*. Mankato, MA: Creative Paperbacks, 2015.

Dobson, Clive. *Wind Power: 20 Projects to Make with Paper*. Richmond Hill, ON: Firefly Books, 2010.

Doeden, Matt. *Finding Out about Wind Energy*. Minneapolis, MN: Lerner Group, 2014.

Websites

Visit the website below to learn about different careers in wind power:
www.bls.gov/green/wind_energy/wind_energy.pdf

Find out more details about wind energy at:
www.windenergyfoundation.org/interesting-wind-energy-facts

Discover the evolution of wind power with this interactive map:
www.gwec.net/global-figures/interactive-map

Capture energy from the wind and see if you can light up the town with this game:
http://climatekids.nasa.gov/power-up

Index